COMMUNICATION MISTAKES
COUPLE MAKES

What happy couples do well

And what unhappy couples do wrong

By

Emily Dixon Ph.D.

Table of Contents

CHAPTER 1

TOWARDS THEORY OF LOW-QUALITY, HIGH-STABILITY COUPLES

On what makes marital happiness and what factors predict divorce, marriage research has surrounded these two questions. But looking only at what makes happy couples happy and what factors cause unhappy couples to break up avoids looking at couples who may be unhappy in their relationship and yet choose to stay together. These couples have been largely viewed as dysfunctional or even as a form of male domination over women. This book suggests that couples who are stable in their relationship, yet are not happy with it, may have something positive to teach us about the dynamics of marriage that has been previously overlooked.

Marriage research has centered on two main constructs: marriage quality and marital stability. Marriage quality has been understood primarily as the independent variable, the variable of process that leads to an end state of stability or instability. Such variables as adjustment, happiness, satisfaction, and commitment have been studied as examples of high quality and are often used interchangeably. Stability, on the other hand, has typically been the dependent variable and has usually been viewed as dichotomous: unstable or stable. A stable marriage is one that is intact until the death of one spouse. An unstable marriage is one that ends in divorce, desertion, or annulment or has been interrupted by separation. This point of view posits that if the marital quality is low enough, the stability of the marriage will be threatened, making stability dependent upon the level of perceived quality in the marriage.

Typologies are a way of trying to understand patterns and trends so that predictions can be made about other couples in other settings beyond the ones under study. One that has stood the test of time was articulated by Lewis and Spanier. They researched 300 articles on marriage quality and stability and analyzed their contents, research variables, and conclusions. Their theory, based upon social exchange, suggests four possible "types" of marriages:

1) high-quality, high-stability (HQHS),
2) high-quality, low-stability (HQLS),
3) low-quality, high-stability (LQHS),
4) low- quality, low-stability (LQLS).

Low Quality
High STABILITY

High Quality
High Stability

Low Quality
Low Stability

High Quality
Low Stability

Figure 1. Lewis &Spanier's couple typology

The first type is those couples that are happy and satisfied with their relationship (high quality). They tend to rarely divorce (high stability). The second type is those couples high in relational satisfaction, but who divorce anyway. This category is understandably small. The third type has low satisfaction with their relationship but still stays together. The last type is those who are both unhappy with their relationship and separate or divorce (low stability or unstable). When Lewis and Spanier wrote their summary article about this proposal they stated that in America roughly 25% of the marriages were of the HQHS category with 50% of the marriages in the LQLS category. The latter category is often calculated from the divorce rate. That leaves about 25% of the couples who are in stable but low-quality marriages. Lewis and Spanier believed that this latter category would decrease in the years toward 2000, whereas the categories of HQHS and LQLS would increase. They seemed to base this conclusion on an assumption that the divorce rate would increase in the intervening years.

But recently many couples who divorce may start HQLS and then rapidly degenerate into LQLS. It may be that for some of these couples the relationship was never stable. This contention is also supported by recent research with 947 engaged, cohabiting, and married couples in which 92.5 percent of the sample said they were "happy" to "perfectly happy" with their marriage!

This kind of result is puzzling though not uncommon in surveys on marital happiness. With a divorce rate hovering in the 40 to 55% range, how can so many couples be so happy yet so many couples be at risk for marital failure? First, we would suggest that most of those older couples in the survey who are happy together are probably at very low risk for divorce. They have made it through hurdles in life that many younger couples will not survive.

Our interpretation of this finding is that, on any given day, most people are happy in their marriages. However, for couples who are at greater risk of divorce, there is a steady erosion of the foundation of their marriage for years that culminates in what appears to be a fairly rapid process of disintegration. In other words, a marriage failing underneath the surface of the hill that does not become apparent until a big enough rainstorm hits (stress in a marriage) to bring the whole hill sliding down. This interpretation would be consistent with other research on what erodes a marital bond over time.

This still leaves the dynamics of the third type; LQHS. These couples can weather disruptions to their marital quality yet remain stable. While it could be that many of these couples are also experiencing a "steady erosion of the foundation of their marriage for years", others may plateau or even improve in their marital quality over time. Stability for these couples may be a prerequisite for marital quality instead of the other way around.

Individual Attempts to Solve the "Unhappy Marriage" Syndrome

Divorce trends have at least followed the prediction regarding low-quality, low-stability marriages. This is the type that typically divorces. Recent statistics indicate that although the divorce rate leveled in the late eighties, in the nineties it is on the way up again, with estimates of 60% to as high as 75%.

As expectations for a "happy" marriage continue to be propagated as the ideal, being in an "unhappy" marriage is increasingly being seen as dispensable. The cultural norm, which used to be "better to remain married even if you are unhappy," has been switched to "if you are unhappy in your marriage, divorce. You deserve better."

This value system, that marriage is expendable if one isn't happy, is propagated not only in the popular culture but by the research community itself. For example, some advocates for victims of domestic violence see divorce as the solution of choice to deal with this issue.

Remaining in an abusive relationship is viewed as an abdication of a woman's dignity as a person and dangerous as well. While few would argue that a person should stay in the same household in threatening circumstances, these researchers suggest that the only way for the woman to get back on her feet again is to divorce and start over. They deny that intervention for male batterers is of benefit or that battering relationships should be saved. This view is held despite the evidence of other researchers that suggests most family violence is committed by young men in their teens and twenties and that it vastly decreases in the thirties and by the fifties virtually disappears.

Thus, by not looking at the entire lifespan, many people are cashing in their relational chips, when many of these relationships might have been safe over time. This does not even take into consideration that much research shows that many batterers can be helped not only to quit battering but also to change their patterns of psychological abuse as well.

The idea that if you are unhappy you should divorce has not borne very much fruit. Studies continue to show the long-term negative effects of divorce. These effects reach into all comers of our society. Even advocates of divorce have a hard time concluding that divorce is a positive thing. There are too many people involved. Divorce is not just a dyadic situation. Many divorces involve children.

They suffer more difficult obstacles in school, future relationships, and self-worth. Divorced fathers have much higher incidences of suicide, accidents, and psychological breakdown. Women suffer primarily in terms of economics, as their incomes typically are lower and often support from their former spouse is not forthcoming. The economic impact of divorce is staggering as couples that could barely survive on their combined salaries now try to support two households.

A common solution to this economic nightmare is to remarry, so that again there can be two wage earners in the house. This is not always a positive solution as the divorce rate for second marriages (often called "rebound marriages" due to the remarriage happening too soon after the divorce) is even higher than for first marriages.

The problems of stepfamilies are complex. It is just not a matter of different people living together. Children from the respective families have divided loyalties, as children usually love both their parents. To see mother or father sleeping with someone other than their parent may be an unsettling experience. That incidents of child sexual and physical abuse and incest are higher in stepfamilies because of the lack of a filial bond and the mores attending to that tie is often ignored.

Another commonly accepted solution to divorce is to cohabit. With divorce so high in our culture, it is easy to understand why young people would choose this option. The argument is that they should see if the two of them are compatible before getting married. What they end up testing is to see if they will be happy. Since the majority of couples in our society are not happy and many are seeking a divorce, can we expect that couples who cohabit will be happier without commitment? Commitment is a high correlate in stable marriages.

Yet our culture views commitment as the culprit. Couples say, if we do away with the "license" and build on altruistic love, isn't that all we need?" Studies have suggested otherwise. Love, or dedication, is only one type of commitment. Without the commitment to the community, the trend toward breakup is even stronger. Both dedication commitment (love) and social commitment (marriage, the support of relatives and friends, government, community, and religious approval) are necessary.

While it is true that social commitment used to be enough to keep couples together, today the role of dedication commitment is growing due to the fragmentation of modem society. Perhaps an explanation of why the divorce rate has skyrocketed in the last thirty years is the wholesale abdication of social commitment as a viable glue to hold people together and the adoption of the idealistic "love" or "happiness" as its replacement.

Are Marriages Worth Saving?

Forgotten in this debate are the time-tested benefits of marriage. Marriage is instinctual, habit brought forth custom that resulted in marriage becoming a social institution with corresponding laws.

While marriage may differ from culture to culture, the basic unit of a man and woman together sharing sexual intimacy, protection, economic resources, nurturance, and procreation and bound by cultural traditions is the general rule. Indeed, commitment to one person of the opposite sex beyond the procreation period is widely found in lower primates.

There must be a reason that marriage has withstood the test of time.

The benefits of marriage are far-reaching. Over and over again, those in marriage fare better than those who divorced or remained single. For example, suicides and homicides are lower for married people than for single, divorced, or widowed people.

Married people smoke less, drink less, and have lower levels of mortality than do single people. When compared to married men, divorced males are twice as likely to die prematurely from hypertension, four times as likely to die prematurely from throat cancer, twice as likely to die prematurely from cardiovascular disease, and seven times as likely to die prematurely from pneumonia.

In a review of the benefits of marriage, married people had fewer problems with alcohol, were more satisfied, had higher incomes, had fewer children dropping out of school, had less poverty, and had a higher hourly wage than either cohabiting people or those in one-parent families, separated, or divorced. Although both sexes who were married live longer, the benefit for men was proportionately higher than for women. It has been suggested that single or divorced men may be prone to more risky behavior than are married men and that unmarried men are more detached from familial responsibility than are corresponding unmarried or divorced females.

The lower mortality rate for both married sexes may be due to the higher financial resources available to married people versus those who are single or divorced. These findings are strengthened further when it is realized that these effects are true for both African-Americans and whites and that mortality rates drop for both races the longer the marriage. Note that widowed women have lower mortality rates than single or divorced women, even when controlling for income.

The benefits of marriage supersede those of living together. The National Institute of Mental Health show that cohabiting women have rates of depression that are more than three times higher than married women, and more than twice as high as other single women. And married people each report significantly higher physical and emotional satisfaction with their sex lives than singles, including those who cohabit.

Although some might argue that marriage is self-selective for the psychologically healthy, the positive effect of marriage on well-being is strong and consistent, and the selection of the psychologically healthy into marriage or the psychologically unhealthy out of marriage cannot explain the effect.

It may be that marriage itself produces certain qualities necessary for improving the quality of life. Lifelong commitments produce trust, sacrifice, relational skills, negotiation and compromise, and an obligation to others. These traits keep a rein on high-risk behaviors and promote the well-being of the family unit, which in turn has a positive impact upon the individual. These benefits of marriage to the individual compound in positive effects upon society at large.

Deficit Models

A popular assumption in contemporary research is that low-quality couples have nothing to offer in terms of positive functioning that could be utilized by others. Instead, it is assumed that if a couple or spouse is not satisfied with their marriage, something must be wrong either with the person or the relationship. If a couple experiences low-quality they have been called dysfunctional.

If one of the spouses is abusive and they stay married, the abusive spouse is often viewed as controlling and power-hungry, while the abused spouse is often referred to as dependent or a victim. Dependency in these settings is viewed as a negative trait. The dependent spouse is often encouraged to become independent instead. Unfortunately, much advice that uses this language leads to divorce despite the desire of many spouses to be able to work out the situation.

But the tendency to divorce as a solution for problems is not only seen in instances of abuse. In our culture, almost any excuse can be given to justify divorce and most are accepted by peers and society as legitimate. For example, if a spouse has any kind of a personal problem, whether it be depression, gambling, drinking, or other so-called "addictive" behavior, the solution of choice for many has become divorce. The belief in these circumstances is that the person with the problem behavior deserves it. The person with the problem is preventing the self-actualization of others, so he or she becomes expendable.

This view is supported even though there may often be a relational element that led to the problem in the first place.

While this systemic view is often accused of casting blame upon innocent bystanders, it is instead a way to look at the problem holistically and to begin to bring healing to the whole family system, not just the injured parties. Thus, divorce, with its lifespan stage-ending finality, also brings to an end the ability of the system to deal with the problem in a healthy way for all the family. The divorced spouses go on other relationships, bringing with them the same issues that they did not deal with in the previous relationship. Abusers tend to abuse other women, abused women tend to pick other men who abuse them. This hardly solves the problem of abuse or other hurtful behavior and only extends it beyond the original family system into yet other family systems!

Rather than pointing out the distressed couple's vast deficits in comparison with happily married couples, one wonders if it wouldn't be more profitable to explore with the couple their reasons for staying together to date, the reasons they were initially attracted to each other, and things that they feel are going OK, even though they have perceived problems in certain areas.

Perhaps what they would tell us would be rather sketchy or illusive. Perhaps with their negative view of the relationship, it will be difficult to ferret out strengths or shared goals or any sort of mutual admiration. But we may learn something about why these couples are going against the cultural norm and staying married even though they are not happy. And maybe what they have to say will help us better understand the true meaning of commitment and sacrifice. Maybe, just maybe, happiness is not the measure of all things.

Why Some Unhappy Couples Stay Together

What constitutes a LQLS marriage? For this book, it is a marriage where one or both of the partners is unhappy with the marriage, yet the marriage is stable over time; that is, they have decided as a couple to remain married. The keyword here is decided; staying in the marriage is a mutual choice of each partner.

Research on domestic violence and recent studies on the physiology of male abusers suggests that there may be a category of marriages low in quality and high instability, but not stable by the choice of one partner. This would involve marriages where the situation is so explosive that the less powerful spouse, usually the wife, feels it would be dangerous to stay lest leaving create worse abuse or even murder. In these circumstances, the abused partner feels powerless and maybe even forced to remain in the marriage despite endangerment.

Some habitual abusers are unemotional in their abuse and unlikely, if ever, to change their lifestyle pattern.

The research on why some low-quality couples stay together is sparse. Usually, those reasons are couched in negative terms or must be implied from studies on why people divorce. A look at the literature on stability reveals that most studies assume that stable couples are happy. The assumption is made that certain factors predict stability and their opposites predict divorce.

The effect of children upon marital stability shows that younger children in the home tended to keep couples together while older children or children born before the marriage increased the chances of disruption. Couples who share the same religious convictions, go to church regularly, and believe in the Bible tend to have lower divorce rates. The issue of wives working and its effect upon stability is mixed.

It depended upon whether or not the wife worked more than her husband or whether her employment status had improved during the marriage. If so, this tended to hurt stability.

Male unemployment hurt stability. Premarital factors affecting stability have often been cited. For example, parents' divorce, the age at marriage, and cohabitation are all predictive of divorce. Lower education of wives, religious heterogamy, and educational heterogamy also decreased marital stability.

Although these SES factors may explain some of the variance in why marriages remain stable, there are other personal factors to consider. Commitment is a salient issue in the divorce-stability domain. If a partner is ambivalent about their relationship, divorce is more predictable. They found that if partners have come to the point where they recommit themselves to the relationship, stability is more likely.

Couples low in fondness for their spouses, low in viewing their struggle as positive, low in seeing their marriage as a team, and high in negative emotions, had a high incidence of divorce 3 years later. Conversely, it might be concluded that couples who liked each other, saw each other as a team, worked together in their common struggle, and had positive interactions would have stable marriages.

An interesting source of information on the stability of low-quality marriages might come from research on long-term marriages. What do they perceive keeps them together so long? The common notion that marital quality is curvilinear (happy in the beginning, a struggle during the child-bearing years, and higher in quality in the empty nest years) may suggest that LQHS couples tend to work out their differences over time and end their year happier than they were earlier. The argument that studying long-term marriages biases the research sample since unhappy couples had previously divorced misses the point that not all long-term marriages were happy all the time!

This happiness in later years is in part developmental, as spouses expectations of each other match the reality of the situation closely. For example, a study on 100 couples over 65 years of age who had been married 45years or more and found remarkable similarity in world views, expectations, commitment to marriage and each other, use of humor, friends, and decision making. Indeed, these couples said they liked each other! Is it possible that all these couples were always HQHS? Is it not possible that there had been some who spent a major

part of their married life at odds, yet finally found
peace with each other?

Re-conceptualizing Stability

Questions for consideration in conceptualizing stability emerge as one wrestles with the theoretical and conceptual meaning underlying the construct.

This researcher questions the assumption made by most prior attempts at constructing theories of marital stability that stability is a static concept represented by the mere fact that a marriage is intact It seems plausible that the construct of stability, like the construct of quality, is continuous rather than dichotomous.

Also, stability is viewed in this book as a dynamic construct, with an ebb and flow of movement along the continuum. Clinically, marriage and family therapists have long contended that every marriage has cycles of tranquility and turbulence and that the degree to which an observer might attribute qualities of stability or instability simply reflect different vantage points of when and how the observer is gathering the data. Viewed systemically, relationships are calibrated by an internal governor that regulates the degree of change and continuity necessary for the survival of the marriage. The concept of stability represents a theoretically more primitive or basic construct that is a requisite condition for the endurance of the system.

The concept of quality, on the other hand, assumes a level of stability as a prerequisite condition for viability. Stability is conceptualized as a basic need that forms the foundational structure and supports the emergence of the construct of quality, which can be assumed to develop as a higher-order level of need.

CHAPTER 2

UNDERPINNINGS

The approach taken in this book borrows from several theoretical orientations to explain why some low-quality marriages are stable.

Social exchange

This theory posits that as long as rewards exceed costs in the relationship, it will remain stable. Four concepts common to social exchange theory relevant to the discussion are commitment, expectations, reciprocity, and choices.

Commitment. Researchers divide commitment into two constructs: constraint and dedication. *Constraint* means those aspects outside the relationship that encourage the stability of a relationship such as religious values, encouragement from family and friends to stay married, commonly shared financial investments, children, and grandchildren.

Dedication commitment, on the other hand, includes internal aspects of the relationship that keep the commitment strong such as sacrificing for the good of the relationship. Thus, social exchange postulates that to the extent that the exchange of commitment (both constraint and dedication) is similar between marital partners, there will be stability.

Although constraint commitment and stability may appear on the surface to be similar or identical constructs, constraint commitment is viewed as a necessary condition for stability in LQHS marriages to occur. However, it is only one of several conditions necessary.

Expectations. Research on expectations has indicated that similar expectations promote stability, but expectations are not static. Different stages in life affect the expectations one has for oneself and one's mate. As time passes, the process of reappraisal of expectations finds new contextual anchors to establish meaning. LQHS marriages, it is plausible that both partners shift their expectations (and share these shifts both nonverbally and verbally) so that both expect few effective interactional rewards while, at the same time, both expect more rewards from extra-dyadic commitments, such as jobs, parenting, hobbies, and ties to friends and extended family. These extra-dyadic commitments may or may not be jointly pursued. For example, a couple may remain married because they don't want to change their shared relationship with their children and grandchildren.

Reciprocity. Reciprocity has been applied commonly to dyadic relationships.

Reciprocity is the notion that the more similar are the perceived exchanges between two people (in this book: husband and wife), the more harmony in the relationship.

Reciprocity in long-term relationships does not have to be like for like and can include either extrinsic factors (e.g., helping) or intrinsic factors (e.g., faithfulness).

Choice. Choice is a major construct of social exchange. While social exchange would predict that people make choices based upon the highest reward for them personally, these personal choices do not always benefit dyadic relationships, individual choices may affect long-term marital stability positively or negatively. Negatively, many relationships are on the verge of breakdown due to the choice of one partner to do such things as drink excessively, engage in domestic violence, or participate in an affair. Conversely, decisions to remain faithful, with no regard for personal sacrifice, may enhance marital stability.

Lifespan

There is a curvilinear relationship of satisfaction over the years of marriage with a dip in satisfaction occurring with the onset of children and going up again when the children leave the home. Lifespan typically has been conceived as the study of the change in individuals over a lifetime. The marital relationship, however, is also developmental. Two concepts of life-span theory are suggestive: plasticity and multi-directionality.

Plasticity. Plasticity is the ability of a person to adapt to changing circumstances and to make up for deficits, either through outside intervention or through compensating in other areas.

Thus, a husband and wife may be unhappy with their relationship but satisfied in other areas that make up for the relational deficits. Some other examples of dyadic plasticity include forgiveness, a refocusing of one's life, or a common vision of a future life together.

Multidirectionality. Multidirectionality is the idea that throughout the lifespan people vary in the direction of their functioning. A young person may be better at remembering short-term memory lists than is an older person, but an older person may be better at applying knowledge to life(wisdom). Applied to couples, multidirectionality suggests that the needs and abilities of individuals in the marriage may change over time.

Even though the individuals change, they may still function well as a couple. For example, early in marriage, couples may downplay individuality, yet in long-term marriages of low-quality individuality may be a crucial element. One could theorize that there are other variations of multidirectionality over the lifespan, such as the amount and style of sexual involvement.

Ecological theory

The advocates of this theory hold that the systems one is a part of influence development. Life circumstances such as health status, employment opportunities, economic resources, educational obtainment and knowledge, race, social class, larger geopolitical forces such as war, economic recessions, and depressions or prosperity, crime rates, and quality of environment, have an impact on marital quality and/or marital stability.

These life circumstances may be key factors that serve as contingency conditions for appraisal of marital quality and marital stability. Marriage and family therapists talk about reframing problems into challenges and opportunities for continued growth and change.

Could it be that couples in LQLS marriages are applying this principle in their reappraisal of life circumstances that impact their marriage relationships?

Social construction

There is a tenant of social construction that may be helpful in this discussion. The basic idea of social construction is that we all construct our reality and it is real for us. This is a helpful orientation in therapy as it gives the therapist the motivation to try to comprehend the reality of the client as he or she sees it. It also serves as a check for the therapist to be ethically aware of his or her presuppositions and worldview and how this client-therapist relationship creates in and of itself another new reality.

HQHS couples are propagated as the ideal, an ideal that many may not be able to ever reach. Or, maybe this ideal is something within reach, if the steps to get from LQLS to LQHS and eventually, even to HQHS, can be reached as a process. Even if the study of LQHS couples creates little that is pragmatic for other couples, social construction would posit that their view of reality deserves to be heard in its own right.

Solution-focus

A particular therapeutic stance that grew out of "social construction" philosophy is solution-focused therapy. Deficit models abound in marital research when it comes to suggesting to low-quality couples how they might improve their marriage. Solution-focus, particularly with a cybernetic bent, suggests instead that rather than look at the problems, we ought to look at the strengths. The cybernetic angle implies that trying to solve the problem is often part of the problem and that something out of the ordinary may be needed instead.

The solution-focused approach asks couples to look at what they are doing right and to concentrate on those. The theory also suggests that little changes bring about big systemic changes. The cybernetic view suggests, also, that systems heal themselves.

This theory combined with lifespan, would seem to bear this out, that given enough time, most marriages can become "happy enough" to make it worthwhile to stick through the difficult times. Unfortunately, many marriages are self-destructing before the cybernetic forces can bring about resolution. But the cybernetician would assume that even the marriages that are both low in quality and low instability have inherent strengths that be tapped as long as the intervention is not "more of the same".

CHAPTER 3

THEORETICAL PROPOSITIONS

To assure precision in the development of this theory, the following propositions are suggested regarding LQHS couples:

I. Stability is time-dependent: the more time the couple is together, the greater the stability.

II. The longer the marriage, the more probable that the LQHS marriage will increase in quality. That is, the relationship between quality and stability in an LQHS marriage is stochastic in time and developmentally dependent.

III. As constraint commitment increases, the probability of marital stability increases. Marital stability for an LQHS couple is contingent upon constraint commitment, not dedication commitment.

IV. The greater the perceived equality in exchange between spouses (reciprocity), the greater the likelihood that a low-quality marriage will remain stable.

V. As the relationship changes and expectations of one or both spouses are not met, one or both will likely adjust their expectations and thus increase the likelihood that the marriage system will remain stabilized.

VI. The more the changes in expectations and choices of spouses are congruent, the greater the probability that marital stability will remain at the status quo level.

VII. The greater the individual plasticity in one or both spouses, the greater the likelihood a low-quality couple will remain stable.

VIII. As multidirectionality increases, stability increases. That is, to the extent that couples can replace areas of deficit with pluses in other areas, their stability will increase.

IX. The greater the life continuity in extra-familial sectors of life, such as employment, housing, and lifestyle, the greater the probability that marital stability will increase over time.

Those couples who can maintain high constraint commitment levels and high plasticity about adjusting to life's challenges and partners' foibles may see the quality of their marriages improve overtime. For example, most couples begin their marriage being happy. Stability is low for all couples in the early stage because constraint commitment, developmentally controlled, has not had a chance to grow. As couples spend time together and make decisions together, their constraint commitment grows (engagement, marriage, children, purchasing of first home).

Because of the high volatility in the early part of marriages, however, as these couples sort each other out and adjust expectations, the first few years are a bit rocky. For some, the trend toward instability and divorce follows a straight line along with a decline in marital quality, as evidenced by the mean age of divorce in the United States of 7.2 years. During this period, many couples divorce.

Those who weather this period begin to build a solid stability, greatly lowering their odds of divorce for each year they spend together. Marital quality lags for LQHS couples, but both constraint commitment and stability continue their upward trend. The difference between stability and marital quality in the area of discontent As long as marital quality lags behind marital stability, satisfaction in marriage will below. As the propositions above explain, over time some LQHS couples can close this gap. This would occur for various reasons such as developmentally through maturity, adjusted expectations, congruence on individual choices, and mutually enjoyable constraint commitment (like the success of their children or grandchildren).

Thus, this model proposes that some LQHS couples, if they can stay together for the course, will migrate toward higher-quality marriages toward the end of the life cycle. The model shows also that some LQHS couples will not improve in marital quality over time, yet still choose to stay married.

CHAPTER 4

INTERVIEWS

This book investigates what keeps couples who are unhappy in their relationships together. To do this, Interviews were conducted with 9 married couples.

These 9 couples were married for 5 or more years (2 were married for 5 years, 1 each for 7,9, 10, 14, 22, 27, and 31 years), who were chosen for the research project. Five years of marriage gave the couple a long enough time to show their stability and to have had enough time to make some adjustments in their marriage.

The goal was to determine what LQHS couples would say are the factors that they believe keep them together.

Couple Analysis

Couple #1. Jim and Debbie, married 27 years. *"Roll with the punches." (Jim)*

Each couple used in this research faced difficult circumstances at the beginning of their relationship. Some couples were able to overcome those obstacles. Unfortunately, the issues that Jim and Debbie had to grapple with at the beginning of their relationship continued to plague them throughout their marriage. This stemmed largely from Jim's tendency to make decisions without consulting his wife. She disagreed with nearly every career decision Jim had made right from the beginning of their time together. The career decisions were dramatic and affected the entire family as they initially had to move. They did this several times until they finally settled on fanning.

Yet the career issue was still confronting them at the time of the interview. Jim felt that they were not making the kind of money they needed to retire, so he was in the process of starting a side business that would be a corporation. His wife felt he was already overworked and underpaid in his work as a farmer. She barely saw him now. If he took on another side business she'd see him even less. He needed his wife's signature on the corporation papers and even though she vehemently disagreed with his new venture she reluctantly signed the papers.

Debbie was frustrated by the lack of partnership between them. She had hoped for a marriage where both of them would work together and share equally in the relationship. Her idea included such things as sharing decision making, sharing household duties, validating each other's feelings, connecting emotionally, spending time together, and sharing common goals.

Over the years these aspirations were largely unfulfilled.

On the other hand, Jim retained his view, which he admitted he inherited from his parents, that the husband has the final say. He said, "Somebody has to be the boss." He felt his wife should come home from her job at night and take care of the chores around the house.

She should keep her nose out of his affairs; "She better not give me hell for the way I operate."

These two conflicting ideas on roles kept the couple apart. They did not connect emotionally, they did not demonstrate much affection for each other nor did they spend time together or share much in common. So what kept this couple together?

Both of them had a wider purpose than their happiness. Jim was making his career decisions with the benefit of the entire family in mind. Both of them suggested that a major factor in keeping them together was their children. Debbie admitted, however, that while this was a major factor earlier in their relationship, she was ready to spend time with Jim and enjoy life together, to build that partnership that had eluded them.

Jim, however, still seemed preoccupied with their financial situation and was trying to recover from the farm crisis of the 1980s that had been a major setback for them.

This wider purpose was also seen in their use of clichés, which had a particularly

Midwestern feel. The idea of "rolling with the punches," "just do it," and "life goes on" reflected their belief that one's responsibility is to make the best of what one has or has been given. Complaining does no good. Divorce is not an option. That wouldn't be rolling with the punches. That wouldn't be an optimistic view of life. Negative feelings are to be put in the right place. If feelings counter one's responsibility, they are to be ignored. "There are no downs." "It's all between your ears." "It all works out in the end." "You forget the downs." "You just kind of keep trying to do the best you can do and hope everything works out." Endurance was a value in its own right that kept them going even when the chips were down, even when they faced incredible odds, even when they disagreed about the most fundamental issues.

However, clichés can prevent intimacy from occurring. In this instance, the clichés have worked better for Jim than for Debbie. It's no surprise she used fewer of them than Jim did. She may have been able to "just do it" but she was unable to "roll with the punches" and pretend it didn't bother her. Jim felt Debbie should just relax and enjoy life instead of letting her different views of his choices bother her. As he said, "no sense both of us worrying."

Despite Jim's seemingly rigid stance on "roles," he suggested that he was more open to Debbie's suggestions and ideas than he was in earlier years. He said he listened to her thoughts on things more and if she had a good point he considered that when making the final decision. That responsibility still fell with him. Debbie suggested that over the years she had become more assertive with Jim about her feelings.

Despite the disparity this couple had in decision making and the resulting sense that they lacked a feeling of partnership, they did not feel they had a bad marriage. When asked his attitude toward marriage Jim said, "When it comes right down to it, it's just a lot between your ears." That is, what makes a good marriage depends upon one's attitude.

Keep a positive outlook, which he felt he had, and all will be fine. He said, "We didn't have many rough times...It's all been up; there aren't any downs. You forget the downs." Debbie said, "We love each other. We respect each other, most of the time. He probably disagrees with that I guess I wouldn't say we have a bad marriage. I wouldn't say that. I think we could have a better marriage."

Couple #2. Mike and Kelly, married 10 years. *"Either deal with them (her husband's resentments) or move on." (Kelly)*

While Jim and Debbie disagreed throughout their relationship on the issue of career choices, Mike and Kelly have struggled with different opinions on how many children they want. Because Mike had been married before and had a child from that marriage, he knew how time-consuming children could be. He had an idea in his head when he fell in love with Kelley, that they would have some time together, just the two of them, to bond as a couple before having children. He was horrified when he found out that Kelly was pregnant 10 days before their wedding. As a result, he wanted Kelly to have an abortion.

When Kelly found out she was pregnant, she was thrilled and thought Mike would share her enthusiasm. Imagine her despair when she heard Mike's request. While Mike interpreted the presence of children as a threat to the relationship, Debbie could not imagine anything else that could bind a couple together more than having children.

The couple did not discuss how they decided for Kelly to go through with the abortion, but it was apparent by the tone of the interview 10 years later that the effects of that situation were still being felt. Mike didn't ever seem to warm up to the idea of having children, not just because of the competition for affection from his wife, but also because of the financial strain. They had decided that Kelly would stay home with the kids. Mike's job was not enough for them to ever get ahead financially, so he felt under constant pressure to work longer hours to make ends meet.

As a result, when Kelly did get pregnant two times later in their marriage, he was not enthusiastic nor supportive of Kelly. This continued to be a blow to Kelly. What can be more invigorating than parents sharing the joy of having children? Indeed, the previous couple expressed that children were a major factor bringing them together. Jim had said, "Everybody's happy when they have a baby and it's healthy." Not Mike. Kelly felt as if he wanted her to feel guilty for having children. She was reluctant to have another child because of the lack of support from Mike, but she desperately wanted to have a baby girl. Just one more go around. Mike wouldn't hear of it. She said she wanted Mike to donate his sperm toa sperm bank so that if anything should ever happen to him and he died, she would go ahead and have her last child.

But this desperate thought was countered by a harsh reality. Her doctors had advised her to have a hysterectomy in the coming year, putting an end to her childbearing forever.

This was hard for her to face. She had to contend with the idea that Mike might even be secretly happy she wouldn't be able to have children anymore which for him would put an end to the issue that had caused so much strife between them. How could Mike empathize with her pain when he never wanted children in the first place?

These kinds of issues often divide couples to the point of divorce. But Mike and Kelley continue to stay married and shared no thoughts of divorce. How can this be?

Kelly said much of it came down to adjusting her expectations downward. She either had to "deal with them (Mike's resentments over their having kids) or move on." By "Move On" she meant divorce. By "deal with it" she was referring to being able to accept the situation despite shattered ideals. Mike, too, felt that acceptance was a critical aspect of their continued relationship. By that he meant giving up the idea that one can change the other and appreciating who the other one was, both the good and the bad. Kelly suggested she had just come to terms with acceptance in the last few months, that she had struggled the previous 10 years of marriage.

Other things that the couple shared that kept them together as a couple were a sense of partnership and shared goals in the relationship, a determination to meet the other's needs, and a willingness to sacrifice for the other and their friendship for each other. While Kelly had changed recently in her attitude toward acceptance, Mike was changing in the way he dealt with conflict. Mike typically kept his feelings inside and did not express them. This kept Kelly guessing and made it hard for Mike to deal with his resentments. Kelly said they argued shortly before the interview where Mike yelled to get his point across. This both startled and pleased Kelly. She was startled because it was unusual for mike to be so adamant. She was pleased because both of them were able to deal with the issue and put it behind them.

Couple #3. Bruce and Wendy, married 5 years. *"Do what you're supposed to do and hang in there."* *(Wendy's feeling of what God was saying to her in her prayers)*

Bruce and Wendy also faced a major difficulty in their early marriage, but unlike the two previous couples, they were better able to put the issue behind them and grow in the area of concern. Bruce and Wendy had a difficult time understanding the different ways that each dealt with conflict Wendy grew up in an abusive family with lots of fighting. In Bruce's family, everything was fine on the surface.

No one argued. So when Wendy let Bruce know her wishes, he didn't know quite how to react. His overly idealized image of marriage was that his wife would meet all his needs and that they would never fight. When his wife proved incapable of meeting all his needs and made demands of her own that countered his desires, he ended up resorting to domestic violence. The couple was not specific on what type or how often that Bruce abused her, but it was a problem for them during their first year of marriage.

Fortunately, the couple found help. Bruce was in his graduate program at the time and Wendy was able to confide in one of Bruce's older classmates who had the wisdom to refer her to Bruce's major professor. The classmate said if Wendy didn't tell the professor about the abuse that he would. This intervention ended up with both Bruce and Wendy in couple therapy where they learned more helpful ways to resolve their differences. The couple indicated that after the first year Bruce was no longer abusive and after the second year he had learned to handle his anger in more appropriate ways.

For both of these partners adjusting their expectations to the reality, they were facing was key to their relationship. Wendy said since her family of origin was not safe she had wanted a marriage that was. When it turned out her young marriage was also not safe she had a hard time facing this reality. How can a person accept that a person you love might intentionally hurt you? No doubt acceptance of this was largely due to both of them being able to make strides in how they treated each other so that the relationship could begin to be safe. Still, Wendy struggled with a loss of trust. It concerned her that even after 5 years she was still not able to trust completely.

But the couple was even more adamant that a key element for them in overcoming this difficulty was their faith. Wendy said she prayed and prayed about the situation with Bruce.

She remarked that her prayers were not just to change Bruce, but to help her see where she had been shortsighted and what could she learn and change that would benefit the relationship. Her pouring her heart out to God gave her an objectivity that enabled her to make changes in her attitudes and behavior.

Bruce suggested that his faith helped him see that as a husband he had a higher calling before God to demonstrate to the world that God was indeed real. If he was a child of God and he beat his wife, what land of a message would that send about the God he worshipped?

This gave him a responsibility not only to his wife but to God and the wider community and as a result, an additional reason to treat his wife kindly and learn to work out their problems together.

This couple emphasized the hope they felt for the future because they had overcome a major obstacle. This created for them a sense of working together. They made a special effort to spend time together and have fun. Bruce felt humor was a key factor that helped them cope. They believed in each other's potential and made efforts to adapt their ways of interacting so that the other would benefit. Thus, Wendy was learning to moderate her confronting style and Bruce was learning to be more forthcoming on things that bothered him.

Wendy also tended to be overly demanding about the way the house was organized.

She was learning to accept Bruce's efforts to help around the house, even though he was not prone to pick up after himself Because Bruce's father just expected his wife to take care of the home front, Bruce had a harder time taking responsibility for household duties. He felt he'd come along way, especially in light of his family background, but both he and Wendy agreed he had a way to go. He attributed his "messy" style to the baggage that came with being in a research doctoral program. If he put his research away he'd tend to have a harder time getting back to it later. When he graduated and had his research office he envisioned he'd do a better job of picking up after himself at home. Wendy was a little more skeptical that he'd make such a drastic change!

Early intervention in this couple's relationship was key in helping them make the changes they need to assure their relationship would be safe. Progress in this area gave them hope that they would be able to make whatever changes were necessary to meet the challenges of marriage in the years ahead. Applying their faith to their lives gave their relationship a higher meaning. Still, spending time together enjoying each other enhanced their relationship.

Bruce and Wendy were interviewed a second time three years later. By that time they had been married 8 years, had their first child, and one other on the way. Each was working part-time with alternating schedules so they didn't need daycare for their child. Both said that their relationship had greatly improved since their fifth year of marriage.

Couple #4. Frank and Shelly, married 14 years. *"If you can put those responsibilities and obligations ahead of your self-interest, you will be a content, self-fulfilled person."(Frank)*

This couple, like Mike and Kelly, had to face the difficulty of an early pregnancy.

The pregnancy was a surprise to them because Shelly had had previous medical problems and she had been told she probably would not be able to have children. When she found out she was pregnant, she saw her baby as a gift fi-om God, a miracle. She was thrilled. Frank's view was similar to Mike's. He didn't want the burden of child-rearing so early in their relationship and told Shelly to get an abortion. Unlike Kelly, Shelly stood her ground against her husband's wishes and said there was no way she would ever do that. It was non-negotiable. As a Catholic, abortion for her was morally wrong. She could not understand how Frank could consider destroying a miracle when it was a gift from God in the first place.

Frank was quite surprised at the strength of her conviction and decided to let her have her way, even though he disagreed. As it turned out.

Shelly could not have any more children, a circumstance that deeply affected Frank. He had made quite a change in his view. He ended up sharing Shelly's enthusiasm. At the time of the interview, they shared that their son Matthew was one of the key joys of their lives.

This couple faced another obstacle early in their marriage. Frank had chosen a career in mass media. This occupation is fraught with a multitude of moves. They moved many times in their first few years together. The moves at first were exciting but then began to take a toll on all three of them. They particularly noticed their son starting to act differently.

They decided that Frank should change careers to something a bit more stable as they noticed that many in the media were on their third and fourth marriages, something they wanted to avoid. They settled on a mid-sized city not far from their respective families and Frank started work in sales where he could be home each evening.

Frank and Shelly were unique in this sample as they were the only couple that divorced each other and then married each other again. Their interview was instructional about the process of separation and remarriage and why they decided to recommit to each other.

Frank said they separated and divorced because he listened closely to the cultural message of the 1980s that emphasize pursuing your happiness. At that time he noticed that he was beginning to be bored with the relationship. He'd been a thrill-seeker in the 1960s and '70s and was a bit put off when his marriage lost its zing. He felt confined in the marriage and decided to go it alone. It was not a mutual decision. He moved out Shelly had to find a small apartment for her and Matthew. Neither Frank nor Shelly made a lot of money (Shelly was a secretary) and they couldn't afford two households. As a single mother, Shelly struggled financially to provide for her and Matthew.

It is interesting to note that Shelly, who often saw herself as not being able to stand up to other's pressure, was being told by loved ones and friends to tell Frank to leave her alone and to learn to depend on herself. She did just the opposite. She still believed in Frank and felt he would come to his senses. So when Frank would stop by to see Matthew, she and Frank would begin to talk. Secretly, she wanted Frank to come back, but she never pressured him to do so, nor did she chasten him for his actions. Frank said that if Shelly had ever told him she wanted nothing to do with him, he would have been gone forever. He secretly wanted to get back together with her, too. He also said that if Shelly had asked to get back together he would have eagerly responded.

As time went on Frank's conscience began to get the better of him. Frank saw Shelly and Matthew in a tiny little apartment with no money to buy the things Matthew needed for school. Frank began to realize he had put his own needs above his family's at his family's expense. He wondered about the relationship between responsibility and personal happiness. Maybe being faithful in fulfilling one's commitments had its rewards that were longer lasting than emotional highs. He started interpreting his actions to divorce Shelly as totally selfish on his part.

Another factor that was instrumental in their remarriage was that he began to attend church for the first time in his life. This was a major change for him, as he had always felt religion was for fools. He made an about-face, joined a church, and even began to teach Sunday school. He asked Shelly if Matthew could go with him to church and she said sure, and so could she. They ended up going to church together regularly. This community involvement gave them an added sense of their higher calling as a couple and both decided to many again.

Shelly said through this whole process she had re-evaluated how she treated Frank. In their early years, she was more timid in how she shared her opinion, notwithstanding her strong stance on abortion. Usually, she was quite uninvolved in discussing issues and decisions with Frank, something that Frank said used to drive him crazy. At first, Frank was threatened by her new assertiveness and even initially used it as one of his excuses to divorce, but now that they are back together he likes her boldness. They both feel they are more in a partnership.

This couple saw themselves in two stages: before and after the divorce. Before the divorce, their relationship was marred by immaturity and selfishness. Shelly said, "I'm not saying we didn't support each other, but neither one of us knew how to pull the other ones good out." Afterward, it was characterized as a compromise, personal and relational change, growth, and teamwork. Frank said that at least for him, he had to come to the place where he realized that love was more than passion: Frank; That's what love is (feeling content like brother and sister). That's another level of a marriage...That's when your relationship is deepening when you know each other so well. Love is not about sex or heat or passion, but about something deeper...!had a spiritual awakening that God calls us to do things and he was calling me to be a man.

And what that means is that men have certain responsibilities, I think...traditional responsibilities toward their women and their children, and they include financial support, spiritual support, all of those things...If you can put those responsibilities and obligations ahead of your self-interest, you will be a content, self-fulfilled person."

Couple # 5. Nick and Angle, married 7 years. *"He didn't feel I was in his comer."*

Mick and Angie also suggested two stages to their marriage. For the first six years, they characterized their marriage as two individuals trying to get the other person to meet their needs. In the second stage, they both began to make an effort to work together as a team, to sacrifice for the other, and to consciously make an effort to meet each other's needs.

Unfortunately, the first stage of their marriage lasted six years. They had a difficult time right from the beginning. On their way to Nick's parent's house to announce their engagement, they found out that Nick's father had tried to commit suicide. Things just seemed to degenerate from there.

Nick had lived a pretty wildlife before seeking to change his life around. He began attending a church and went to the church single's group. That's where he met Angie who led the group. Angle's family were strict fundamentalists who valued keeping everyone comfortable. Mick's family was volatile and valued letting another know if a family member thought something was amiss. Not to do so would be a betrayal. Imagine the conflict between these two styles! Angie interpreted Nick's volatility as an outrage; Nick interpreted Angle's passivity as outright rejection. It took them six years to sort out these different ways of looking at each other.

This problem would have been bad enough, but it was compounded by Nick's physical and mental health. Three months after their marriage he found himself unable to get out of bed and go to work. Nick had been an ambitious and active construction worker for several years before he ever met Angie. It paid very well. He loved his job but now he couldn't even go to work. What was wrong?

No one knew how to handle this, least of all Angie and Nick. Angle's parents pretended on the outside to treat them normal, but soon it became apparent that they could not accept Nick's not going to work. They doubted his faith and sincerity. In their view, a faithful person would not stay home from work. Their church friends also rejected them.

Their friends did not have a place in their arsenal for a person who claimed to be a Christian yet did not fulfill his responsibilities. While Angle struggled, she still thought the best of nick. She said:

Angie: It was scary to me, but...it didn't even occur to me to abandon him or that getting married was a bad idea. I still wanted to be with him I thought that...it would be better for him for me to be with him...I felt like it was temporary; that it could be fixed.

She did not doubt his motives but she was thoroughly confused and did not know what if anything she could do to help. So she did nothing, hoping the problem would just go away. Meanwhile, Mick was feeling his world was getting smaller and smaller. He felt there was no one to help him in his time of need. He began to feel resentment toward Angie for her passivity, believing she was "not in his comer."

It took years before they finally figured out an answer to Nick's lack of energy that was satisfactory enough for them to begin to treat each other as partners. Nick was finally diagnosed with a thyroid problem. When that was treated, his energy level increased.

However, he was still not the same, strong, physical self with whom Angie first fell in love.

They also concluded he had a long-term depressive disorder that had some links to his father's side of the family. Knowing what the enemy was enabled them to regroup and face it together.

But not before a crisis. Nick reached the end of his patience a year before the interview and told Angie he wanted out. He was tired of feeling alone and felt like their marital problems were his fault. He told her if she couldn't be supportive, then they might as well call it quits. They separated for three months, which turned out to be a wake-up call for Angie. Until that time she had taken her parents' cue on how to build a marriage. In her family, people don't work on marriages. It just happens. The family rule also was to not tell others what one thinks because that might hurt them. It was of utmost importance to make sure everyone was comfortable. However, this approach was not working in her marriage.

Nick needed more from her. She realized that she couldn't sit by and let Nick handle his demons alone if she was going to stay married. She was going to have to learn to be assertive, to say her opinion, to challenge Nick's thinking, and to work with him as a partner in solving their problems together. She could no longer sit by and let Nick make decisions without her input. He didn't want to do that nor, in his state of mind, as he always capable of doing it.

At the same time, Nick needed to learn to back off a bit He stated his opinion with such force that often Angie shut down. He needed to be patient with Angie, to give her time to think so she'd be freer to express her opinion.

Angie; We're trying to change the roles so that things that come up in our marriage that..need to be addressed are addressed by both of us and seen as a mutual problem, a mutual situation to work out rather than something that's wrong with him...Taking equal responsibility for working out of things.

At the time of the research interview, Nick and Angie were just in the process of healing from their rough first six years together. They still struggled with the same issues, but there was no longer any doubt that they would be able to solve their problems together.

They had been through a very trying time and had survived. Nick was trying to put his life together despite his lower energy level and had gone back to college to change careers to something a little more sedate than construction. Angie was having a hard time believing he'd be able to finish his schooling as Nick had had a difficult time finishing other things their first years together. Nick struggled with his test level of Angie. Would she be there for him?

Like the other couples in this sample, this couple was fraught with early problems, some of which were still not resolved after seven years of marriage. Certainly, their lack of support from both sides of the family and the loss of emotional support from their church friends isolated the couple and exacerbated their problems. They still have their bitterness to attend to lest they end up isolating themselves from others for the rest of their lives. Yet despite not having an extended support system this couple had shown remarkable resolve. Because both of them were able to adjust their expectations and the way they dealt with conflict, both were confident about facing the future together.

Couple # 6. George and Vi, married 31 years. *"We're not in each other's hair."*

Of the nine couples in this sample, this was the most "married". They had little in common with each other except for their children. They married at a late age (Vi was 37).

George had lost his wife and had three children to tend to. He was looking for a mother to watch over his children. She was in the process of looking for a husband. They described their relationship in almost business-like terms.

Vi said she was an outgoing person who likes to talk to people and have lots of people around her. George liked the outdoors and being alone. That would be fine, except that Vi got lonely if she was out in the country too long. George felt Vi and her friends were nosey and he had no desire to be part of that. This preference extended to their relationship. George felt Vi talked all the time. It drove him "crazy." Vi could not endure George's silence and took it as a personal affront.

They said the key to their relationship was that "We're not in each other's hair."

They meant that literally. George solved their differences by buying a cabin in the woods.

He lived there and she lived in town. They rarely saw each other except for family affairs.

They had separate checking accounts and made separate decisions for their different households. As with most divorced couples, the only time they saw each other was when it involved the children.

Yet this couple refused to divorce. They didn't believe in it. They concluded the only way they could stay married was not to see each other. They both affected the other negatively and neither enjoyed being with the other. George seemed content in the situation although he said, "I wish I had a partner that is more to my way of thinking." Vi expressed hurt in that she would like to be able to go to church with somebody so others would not ask themselves where her husband is. She didn't like going to community functions or dinner alone as she didn't want others to think there was something wrong with her because her husband wasn't with her. Still, her comments didn't suggest that she wanted to be with George because she liked him, but only because of an image she wanted to portray to others that everything was OK. George didn't care what her needs on this matter were. He said if she insisted he go to church or out to eat with all her friends he would divorce her. And that was that. No compromise.

George; I go my way and she goes hers. Otherwise, our marriage wouldn't work. I couldn't live her life and she couldn't live mine...It is either this or two people get a divorce.

So Vi swallowed her pride and put up with the personal disgrace of an absent husband to avoid the worse disgrace of divorce. She made the best of a bad situation and even saw some positive reasons to live the way they did:

Vi: At first I didn't like it, but then I got used to the fact that I can do whatever I want, whenever I want, and I don't have to stop and get a meal. If I want to eat at midnight, I can and nobody cares. If I want to go play bingo, I don't have to rush.

Indeed, they thought in some ways they had a good relationship. Vi said, "I Wouldn't think of going out with another man. I wouldn't be interested in anybody else." And George said,

"We tolerate each other's differences." When they were asked on a scale of 1 to 10, with 1 being none and 10 being complete, where he would rate his relationship with Vi in terms of happiness they said: George: I would say about an eight, seven. It sure isn't perfect, but it isn't all that bad. The fact that we can compromise. It would be plain hell for either one of us if one party insisted this is the way we are going to live.

Vi: But when you get right down to it, like you say about the cabin, you really wouldn't want me there all the time. We are used to being apart and I'd drive you nuts.

George: You can wear a guy a little thin.

Vi: And you can wear a guy thin by being uncooperative. We have learned to compromise. I guess about a seven or eight too.

George: It sure as hell isn't a perfect situation. It's damn expensive for one thing. While on the surface George and Vi's relationship seems artificial and bordering on divorce, the couple still saw that they were being faithful to each other, compromising to accommodate each other's preferences and both shared a commitment to their family. Not surprisingly, this couple had the lowest combined score on the DAS than any other couple in the sample. The couple did have some concerns about how they would handle things when and if either of them became disabled due to old age and failing health. They both concurred they have a hard time being with each other for any length of time.

Couple #7. Tom and Yvonne, married 5 years. *"As long as we have each other everything will be OK." (Tom)*

Yvonne was married and had a daughter before divorcing and meeting Tom. As with the other couples in the sample, there were early problems; financial, problems with her ex-husband, and an early pregnancy before their marriage. Fortunately, Tom was excited about Yvonne's pregnancy so they did not run into the same problems as Mike and Kelly (#2) did where Mike wanted his wife to get an abortion.

Later, Tom and Yvonne had problems due to Tom's stress on the job. He'd take his work problems home with him and as a result, Yvonne felt that he would shut down and ignore her. Also, they had moved to a different state where Yvonne didn't know anybody. It didn't help that Tom worked for his brother and that he put in 60-70 hours per week. This created some problems for them as a couple. What got them through that period was their belief that the situation was only temporary. This hope turned out to be correct as once they moved to a different location with different jobs, the stress level was reduced and their relationship noticeably improved. Yvonne said it was difficult for her to initially trust Tom because she had some hurt leftover from her first marriage. At the time she met Tom she was not looking for a mate and said that "all men were scum" in her mind at the time. She was surprised to find out how kind Tom was-so surprised she couldn't believe it until they had been married some time. She indicated that her trust slowly built over time.

By the time of the interview, about 6 1/2 years after they met, Yvonne said the best thing about their relationship is that they are best friends. She said, "I can tell him anything. Just knowing he was there for me was a real up, because I never had that before."

Tom said for him that the best thing about the relationship was their willingness to sacrifice, to go out of their way to meet each other's needs. He described it this way: Tom: I would do anything for her and she would do the same for me. That means a lot, especially when I had been single for 33 years.

By the time of the interview, they still struggled with their busy schedules and the presence of kids in the family. While the idea of being their own "family" was a really important aspect of their relationship, it also produced a shortage of time together. When they are together they "cherish" the time. They said they used humor to get through stressful times, and tried to be frank with their children when they had disagreements with them.

They believed that they had the most essential element to make a successful marriage, namely, communication. Tom said that "Not being honest is the worst thing you can do."

They strove to keep their communication forthright. They said they have always moved ahead in their relationship by "being positive, having faith...In our relationship, we haven't ever taken steps back. We've always gone forward." Other elements of their positive view of the relationship were that they both work hard in the relationship, have realistic goals, and both give to each other. Making peace with what they have has also contributed to their contentment.

Tom: We don't have that many wants. I think that's good for our relationship, too. Nice things would be nice to have, but they are not necessary. We always say as long as we have each other everything will be OK.

Tom and Yvonne were still new to their marriage and hope was a key element for them. Still, Yvonne indicated that their lack of time alone was a major contributor to her struggle in the relationship.

Beneath the surface, Yvonne said that they both have a steady love for each other.

When asked how Yvonne knew that Tom loved her she replied: Yvonne: Because he cares. He listens to what I say. He cares about my feelings because he takes interest in them. If I'm feeling bad he will make efforts to make me feel better.

Scheduling has given them two lives apart. They each worked different schedules, so it's like they have two different families in one: Tom: It's more like two small families. It is either me and the kids or her and the kids. I am with the kids at night and she is with them during the day.

As a result, they end up doing things as individuals and rarely together. They've made up for this deficit by highly valuing their time together. Another factor that contributes to this working for them is their being able to accept this situation: Tom: I accept that with no major problems. It is not something we want, but we

know that's what we have to do.

Y: At this time. It's not always going to be this way.

Acceptance for them was easier knowing that someday their schedules would change and they would be able to see each other. Knowing that each wants to be with the other and considering each other their best friend would also seem to be factors that would contribute to their acceptance of a potentially harmful schedule.

This couple is forced out of financial necessity to be separated. Because they each knew the other loved them, and they enjoyed each other's company, the time apart created anticipation instead of resentment.

Couple #8. Carl and Eve, married 9 years. *Micro vs. macro-management*

When Carl and Eve met. Eve was on the rebound from a second divorce and had 2children. Carl was surprised that his parents accepted Eve and his decision to marry. Eve's parents were another matter. Because Eve had already divorced twice, they pulled Carl aside and asked him if he was sure he knew what he was doing given Eve's track record!

Shortly after they got married. Eve was pregnant again and her father became ill. She decided to go home to help with his care. She didn't call it going home to help. She called it a "move." During this time they were separated. As a result, Carl wasn't able to be there through her pregnancy. They were shortly to find out that this was a pattern for them.

With two children in the relationship from the start, Carl and Eve had little time together. An added stress over the history of their relationship was that Carl was gone for long periods as his job took him overseas. Eve commented that in their 9 years of marriage, if all of their time together were condensed it would add up to only one year! During his absences.

Eve and the children got into their routine. Then when Carl returned things would get topsy-turvy for a while. Plus, as the children aged and stayed up later, they noticed they had little time for themselves as a couple.

What got them through these long periods away from each other? Eve explained that while it was very difficult, she had faith in their relationship and believed it was going to work. Carl believed that their sharing a child right away sealed the relationship and that if it hadn't been for that he doubted they would have survived these early separations.

They indicated their best time in the relationship was the time alone they spent in Jamaica. In their 9 years together, both said this was a highlight of their relationship. They had little conflict when they are alone together. They struggle more when they had kids to tend to.

Because of their lengthy times away from each other, they found that they had different needs. When Carl came home he was tired of being with his business associates and going out to eat and all he wanted to do was spend time with his wife and the kids. During Carl's absences, Eve was alone with the kids and so she longed to be alone or with adult friends when Carl came home. These different needs were not too compatible and created conflict between them.

They also differed on how they dealt with conflict. Carl was easy-going and tried to avoid conflict. Eve liked to get the issues on the table and then be done with it: Carl; I think there's a recurring problem...!don't respond well to criticism or enjoy conflict and I just don't deal that well with it. Now from my vantage point at least, E. is real good from a macro sense about making adjustments and being accepting, but on a micro-level, I think she likes to control her surroundings and that brings us into conflict quite often...She likes to talk things through and I usually get upset...

Eve: I don't have a problem with conflict. It doesn't phase me in the least. I have two teenagers. We conflict... regularly. It's forgiven and it's done...I don't question the love in the relationship. I don't question the viability of the relationship I have with my children....it's more difficult for him. He's very easy going...He's very calm and that's good because I get off the wall. But it's not a serious thing. I could forgive it in five minutes. He finds that intimidating...

Carl described his philosophy of marriage as being able to give each other "a certain amount of personal freedom." Eve agrees and said that Carl struggled with that because when he came home after a long absence, he wanted Eve to himself; whereas Eve was climbing the walls and ready to explore the world herself. Eve suggested that her philosophy of marriage included being able to "treat each other with respect and to recognize each other's need for...personal space." Carl went on to define what he meant by saying that in a mature marriage each partner would be given space to develop their interests without threatening the relationship. Eve said it would embrace "the differences as opposed to shunning them or asking them to conform across the board." They agreed that while this was a goal, they both tended to be controlling of the other with Eve trying to control day-to-day issues, and Carl was more concerned with controlling the over-arching issues.

Eve emphasized that for her to stay in a marriage it had to be good. She wasn't going to stay in a marriage just to stay in a marriage. Her mother and father were married for a long time. Eve didn't view their marriage as being very rewarding personally; Eve: I don't believe in being with someone just because it is the right thing to do, or appears to be the right thing to do...When I address Carl on our relationship, I remind him I'm there because I want to not because it just is.

Carl anticipated that as the children grow and leave the home that their relationship would improve because they would be able to spend more concentrated time with each other.

Eve was skeptical: Eve: It (the children growing up and leaving home) will enhance certain parts of our relationship, I would think, I would hope. On the other hand, it may be a do or die. We may have time to spend together and it won't work...Who knows? I don't know that.

Later in the interview, when asked about her view of them as a couple in the future, Carl said, "As far as expectations go, I don't know if I have that many, or, any." Eve said, "I just hope that we make it. That's my thing." When asked by the interviewer if she meant survival as a couple or survival in life. Eve replied, "-as a couple."

This comment and the one previous make two that Eve made about her uncertainty in the relationship. This is the only person in the entire study who suggested any doubt about the future of the relationship. For the rest, divorce was not an option. Despite her sharing these thoughts, she said she's secure in their relationship. What was a concern for her, however, was that her husband did not seem to her to be secure in the relationship. Her direct approach to conflict did not just threaten Carl emotionally. In her opinion, she believed that Carl thought her style threatened the relationship.

Couple #9. Harry and Lora, married 22 years. *"I don't know if there are really any major problems."*

Harry and Lora certainly had their share of early challenges to their relationship.

Shortly after their marriage Lora got pregnant, Harry started in the military in South Carolina, and the family moved from the Midwest to an entirely new culture. Not having the support of their extended family during these tender times helped them develop a sense of self-reliance which was difficult, nevertheless. After Harry's stint in the military (he saw no combat), they moved back to Minnesota to live with her folks. Four months was all they could take before they moved out on their own.

After being by themselves across the country, living in the same house with in-laws was too close. Harry eventually went into business with an old high school buddy. They relocated to Wyoming and for several years Harry was on the road tending to the needs of their business. However, his partner took advantage of the situation, and before long Harry was out of the business having lost the money he invested in it. This meant another move and finding new work. Thus, their first few years were filled with time away from each other and frequent moves. After this last move, Harry found work close to home and was now home regularly. But because he had been gone so long it now became difficult for both of them and the children to adjust to Harry being home all the time.

Now the problem became being too close! Another major setback for them was losing a baby at birth. The couple shared that of all the problems they've had, losing their baby was the most difficult for them. Fortunately, they had friends and family who were very supportive.

The hardships this couple faced in their early years seemed to have given them a resilience against letting day-to-day problems get them down. Harry interpreted their life together; Harry; We've had our ups and downs, but our ups and downs and battles haven't been major ones to cause any kind of concerns to even warrant wanting to break it up or anything like that.

Other than this resilience what was their glue? Harry said that they enjoyed each other's company and they were pretty good at communicating with each other. Lora suggested they would do better if they didn't assume what the other was thinking, even though Harry thought that was a possible strength; being able to anticipate where the other was heading. Harry believed, instead, a factor they needed more of was a sense of humor.

Acceptance of the other helped them overcome their differences: Harry; We get our own little problems and our own little quirks. Everybody has that. But we've learned to adjust and how to deal with it and accept or just plain try to forget everything.

When asked how they've changed over the years Lora said she'd become a more independent person due to Harry's long absences. Lora also said she thought that Harry had been able to take other people's (Lora's?) schedules into consideration instead of just making plans without consulting anyone.

When asked what they hoped never changed about their relationship they discussed

their intimacy and faithfulness to each other;
Lora: Probably the closeness, the feeling of
Harry: Always being there.

Lora: Yeah, that's it. We've always been able to rely on each other; support each other whatever...

Harry: That type of thing: just never having to worry, I guess. I've spent a lot of time away from home (and) there would have been more than enough opportunity for Lora and I cheating on both our parts...

Lora; (Did I ever) tell you that Chuck asked me that once, if I worried about (you)when you went out on the road?

Harry: Yeah.

Lora: Oh, did I tell you that?

Harry: Yeah. No, (it) never really enters the mind...More opportunities would have probably been there, you know, easily, if somebody would have been looking for them.

The last statement is instructive. Faithfulness was something they did not worry about because neither of them were out looking for another partner. If they had, the opportunities would have been there. Because they weren't looking they didn't have to face the temptation, nor struggle with wondering if the other was faithful.

CHAPTER 5

CHALLENGES

Five domains were discovered in the data that were characteristics of these couples which contributed to their stability. These couples each faced early challenges to their marriage with which they were able to develop ways to navigate. They also viewed their relationship as primary above themselves as individuals. Some, but not all, of the couples, also viewed their relationship as subordinate to their faith

That is, then* marriage had a wider purpose in God's call on their lives. These couples also believed that there was a general balance in the amount of give and take in the relationship. Most of the couples (7 of 9) saw their ability to adapt to changing circumstances and to adapt the way they interacted as giving them a fundamental hope to face an uncertain future. Finally, these couples demonstrated how expectations need to be adjusted for partners to reach a state of accepting each other and to be open to each other's influence in their lives.

What do the participants say are the key characteristics of their relationship that encourage them to stay together? After investigating their interviews and categorizing the various issues the following domains emerged that encourage stability in low-quality couples.

Domain 1. An ability to survive early challenges to the marriage

Every couple faced early challenges to their relationship which they were able to survive. Only one couple faced just one major challenge. The rest were confronted with multiple challenges. These challenges occurred in three major areas: 1) about the wider economic system; 2) about others outside the marital dyad and 3) about each other.

Relationship to the wider economic system

The nature of the economic challenges had to do with career choices that took partners away from each other, required the couple to move away from their families of origin, or involved long hours of work for little pay. Two couples discussed their disagreement on career choices with the wives believing their husbands made poor choices while the husband defended those early choices. Five couples moved immediately after getting married, one to start a graduate program, one with the military, and two to start new jobs. Several couples reported multiple moves and multiple jobs in those early years as the couple tried to establish themselves. Thus, these couples did not only have to face the difficulty in adjusting to the change in getting married, but they had to adjust to being away from their families and a support system of friends, church and relatives, in a new part of the country, and/or new jobs or new school. This change in the environment, while stressful, for some of the couples facilitated their maturity and self-reliance as a couple, forcing them quickly to leam to cooperate and support each other.

Some of the couples were also separated from each other in the early years. One couple was separated from each other right after they got married due to her father's illness when she went home to care for him. A husband was separated from his wife because of his demanding work schedules and two husbands were on the road constantly and saw little of their wives. As one husband said: "We had some problems with my working several shifts straight and not sleeping at night and just being gone all day. It was a huge problem."

Relationship to others outside the marital dyad

The second major challenge for these couples was in the area of relationships with others outside the dyadic relationship. Five of the couples had a partner who had been previously married. Of these five couples, only one was a single parent due to a spousal death. The rest brought with them the resulting step-family problems of a former spouse and children from that marriage. In all of the previously married couples, there were children involved. All of the couples with former spouses had only one partner who had been previously married.

Thus, part of the adjustment difficulty was for the spouse who had never married. These partners tended to be more trusting of their previously married spouse than their spouses were of them. Those previously married due to divorce mentioned trust issues with their current spouse as a hang-over from being hurt in their first relationship.

This lack of trust was difficult to understand for the spouses who were not married before.

And because of the presence of step-children from the start, there was little time for the couples to bond.

Another relationship that affected these couples early on was that 5 of the 9 couples experienced early pregnancies. Three of these pregnancies were in couples who already had the presence of step-children. Two were pregnant before their wedding, the rest were pregnant within the first year. Two husbands were adamantly opposed to the pregnancies and insisted their wives get abortions. One wife went through with the abortion against her own better judgment; the other wife refused and the child was later viewed by both the husband and wife as a miracle from God, as the wife could only have one child due to health limitations.

Another challenging relationship outside the couple dyad were in-laws. Two couples reported this was a particular problem for them. In both cases, the wives' parents were critical of the husband due to differences in lifestyle. In one of the cases, it was exacerbated by the husband becoming depressed to the point of being unable to work just three months after the marriage. His in-laws interpreted his depression as a spiritual problem and cut him off from their support. Unfortunately, this couple was also cut off from their religious community as their church friends also had doubts about the couple's faith.

Relationship between partners

A final area of early challenges was in the area of conflict between partners. All of the couples reported a different conflict style that was difficult to navigate during those early months together when ideals were high and differences were not anticipated. For one couple, this difference in conflict styles led to domestic abuse. A typical conflict pattern that was described by the couples was one partner pursuing issues and the other withdrawing from the issues. In two couples the husband was the pursuer and the wife was passive. Interestingly, these were the only two couples who experienced the crisis of separation. One of them divorced over this issue (1 year) while the other only separated (3 months). Both couples reunited when they were both able to change their conflict styles, with the husbands learning not to be so forceful in their demands and the wives learning to be more assertive.

In the rest of the couples, the passive person was the husband, and the assertive one was the wife. These husbands reported viewing their wives' assertiveness as attacks on them personally and had difficulty hearing what their wives were saying. As they withdrew to escape conflict or to keep it from escalating their wives saw this as abandoning the relationship and as invalidating what the wives felt were important issues. Thus, these wives often escalated the conflict to get some sort of a response out of their partner.

Health problems plagued two couples. One husband, mentioned above, had a depressive disorder attributed to thyroid problems and his family of origin. Another wife had diabetes whose illness had been a struggle for both of them during their entire relationship.

Still another couple reported they had a handicapped son who needed constant care. This was in the relationship from the beginning, a child of a previous marriage.

One couple (#9) said their biggest challenge was losing a baby at birth. Yet they did not express that this had hurt the relationship. It was a painful thing they both shared, but it was not the fault of anyone. Instead, it gave them a common bond.

Fortunately, this couple had several family and friends who were supportive during this most difficult time.

Surviving the challenges

These couples demonstrated both positive and negative results from these issues.

The biggest negative contribution of these problems was, for some, it tended to define their entire experience as couples and at times appeared to be overwhelming. For example, the couple who experienced health problems for the husband also experienced a cut-off from their friends and family. They also struggled with conflict style differences. The inability to adequately address these issues in the early stages of their relationship led to the loss of trust the couple was still trying to gain when interviewed.

Another couple struggled with separation at the beginning of the relationship due to the husband overworking. Twenty-seven years later the husband's tendency to be gone because of his work was still seen as a major roadblock to their building a quality relationship.

While the wife still hoped for a time when they would spend together, the husband admitted he'd probably work himself into an early grave.

Yet, the majority of the couples reported that they had learned important lessons from the challenges and had even grown together and matured as individuals through them.

For example, while Bruce and Wendy (#3) experienced domestic violence during the first year of their marriage, they were able with counseling, intervention, religious conviction, and personal maturity, to re-pattern the way they dealt with conflict and had been violence-free for 4 years. Being able to change gave them encouragement as a couple and gave them resilience for later disagreements. Several couples reported that moving away from home so early gave them a chance to depend upon themselves and helped them formulate as a couple.

Most of these ended up moving back closer to their families where family support was again an important factor in their ongoing success as couples. The frequent moves for one couple helped them to see the danger for them as a couple and for their child. The husband ended up changing careers so that they wouldn't have to move again and could build more stability in their relationship and family life.

Similar situations had different results, depending on how the couple handled the problem and how they individually viewed the problem and each other. Mike's insistence that Kelly (#2) get an abortion and the resulting abortion began a division between them over children that was still with them 10 years later at the time of their interview. The same situation brought Frank and Shelly together when Shelly refused to get an abortion because of the depth of her religious convictions. Though, at the time, Frank did not share her faith, he found that he did respect her. Over the years the birth of their only son became a unifying factor in their relationship.

While ex-spouses created havoc for those families with former relationships, they also provided an opportunity to unite against a common enemy and to formulate their own identity as a couple. Early problems with step-children seemed to dissipate over time with only one couple having complaints about that aspect at the time of the interview and that was largely due to the child's health difficulties.

Indeed, one couple (George and VI, #6) even said it was the step-children that brought them together, both as a couple initially and during most of their marriage. George and Vi struggled after the children were grown to find common interests, but felt very strongly about how important her role was to George's three children; Vi: The youngest boy loved me to death. He would always sit next to me on the davenport, and he always put his hand on my leg or something and we would go to church and he was nestled up to me, and after he died we saw this thing he had written about his life story, and he said when his dad met me and got married, he thought that was his mother coming back, because he was only 2 years old when she died. He thought I was his mother who came back from the grave I guess.

Several couples reported it was the addition of children to the family that helped them formulate as a couple. One suggested that if they wouldn't have had children, they Wouldn't have had anything to keep them together during those early years. It gave them a common goal, interest, and bond, something they could unite on together.

Those couples that did not have children at the time of the interview looked forward with anticipation (and some fear!)to having children. For each of the couples married 20 or more years, children were a decisive factor in their relationship and now with the onset of grandchildren, family rituals around birthdays, etc., took on new meaning. Indeed, these family events were about the only thing George and spoke fondly of together. These same older couples all struggled with reinventing their relationship with the onset of the "empty nest," but despite disagreement on sometimes quite major issues, they all spoke with fondness of their mutual love and concern for the welfare of their children and their families.

While surviving outside challenges provided the opportunity to bring spouses together against a common foe, if the conflict was between them, the healing had to take a different form. Wendy described how working together on Bruce's domestic abuse helped them recover, yet she was quick to point out forgetting was not an option: Wendy: When we moved here it really started to feel like that was some part of another life. But as I've told Brace, I don't know if in my mind I can honestly say it will ever be gone.

It just leaves something. You know it's almost like your body, once you cut the side you can heal over with scar tissue and can be stronger than it was before, but you see a scar. You notice a scar. It's kind of that way with our marriage. It's healed over and I think for the weakness that it was, it's turned into something very strong, but not unforgettable. So that's kind of how I see it I don't know how to answer you as far as saying we've gone to another stage. I can say emotionally, I feel like I'm in a different marriage, but there's always going to be Utde memory. I can't say that it's completely ever gone.

Domain 2. A philosophy of marriage that emphasizes the bigger picture

These couples discussed how they put their marriages first before their own individual preferences. With this hierarchy of priorities in their lives, divorce became less of an option. All of the couples discussed the elevation of their relationship over individuality.

Two couples said their relationship was also subordinate to their faith.

The elevation of the relationship over individuality

How the couple demonstrated that the relationship was a priority versus their own individual preferences was seen in several ways: their attitude toward divorce, how the benefits of marriage we worth their sacrifice, a viewing of the relationship as primary, and the importance that fidelity and commitment played in protecting the marital bond.

Attitudes toward divorce. Of the 18 people interviewed for this book, only one hinted that divorce might be a possibility. Eve (#8) said that the marriage had to be good or she'd be out of the relationship. She indicated that the marriage was "good" and she felt secure in the relationship as it currently stood.

But she felt that her refusal to say she'd always be in the relationship no matter what caused her husband to be a bit insecure in their relationship. He might have also been insecure because she had already gone through two husbands. Would he be the next? Hanging marital quality over the relationship made him a bit uncertain. What if the couple has a downturn for a time due to health, mental health problems, a death in the family, a lost job, financial disaster, or whatever. Will the couple be able to survive?

But Eve's attitude was remarkable in that it was a solitary voice. The others in the sample remarked instead that the relationship came first before individual whims or situational downturns. This is not to say that divorce or its threat was not on their minds at all. Several of the couples struggled with this question For example, Kelly (#2) said she came to a point of decision in the relationship where she had to decide to either accept her husband's foibles and limitations, including the hurt he had caused her, or "move on." She decided to accept the limitations. Frank and Shelly (#4) did literally divorce at one point only to remarry each other later. At the time of the interview, Frank attributed their original divorce to his own immaturity and selfishness. He believed he had put his own happiness before that of his family, to his own shame.

When he got back together with Shelly, he did so because he had come to the point where he viewed his responsibility to his wife and son as something dignified in its own right. For Mick and Angie (#5) their relationship was at a deadening stalemate until Nick threatened divorce and the two actually separated for three months.

This turned out to be a wake-up call for Angie and she began to take a more active role in the outcome of the relationship. Interestingly, before their separation, Nick had been unable to work due to health and mental health issues for a lengthy period. While others might be tempted to divorce in such circumstances, Angie said, "It didn't even occur to me to abandon him or that marriage was a bad idea."

One couple's relationship seemed to this researcher to be a virtual divorce (#6). The couple lived in separate residences, had their own separate checking accounts, did not enjoy being together, did not look forward to spending time together, and did not have anything in common except their children, much like a divorced couple. Yet this couple did not see themselves that way. They saw themselves as very much married and actually able to compromise. They were willing to not make any demands upon each other so that they could stay married. As George said, "it's either this or 2 people get a divorce," and "I couldn't live her life and she couldn't live mine."

The rest of the couples rarely mentioned divorce. It seemed to be a non-issue. Harry expressed it well (#9): "We've had our ups and downs, but our ups and downs and battles haven't been major ones to cause any kind of concerns to even warrant wanting to break it up or anything like that." Wendy (#3) commented on her fluctuating emotions early in the relationship, during a time where she was being domestically abused; Wendy: And you know it is amazing, through that all despite the intensity of the emotions that were generated through all of the experiences, we still wanted to be with each other.

And that was, I mean there were days like, I do want to be here. I'm scared- But it would last, if we were separated for just a day or two then that was gone, that feeling of need to have to leave or whatever. .My theory even then, though, was I will never divorce this guy.

Never.

Benefits of marriage.

The couples focused on the priority of marriage instead of the benefits of leaving. Marriage had benefits to them that superseded their problems. For a person, like Frank (#4), who grew up in a home where partnership and belonging were not encouraged, being a "normal couple" carried a high value. Frank commented that just doing mundane things like going to the grocery store together meant so much to him. He expressed appreciation for his wife helping him to "settle down." He said, "if there ever was a barbarian who needed to be civilized it was me." He also liked the idea of knowing someone really well and having the opportunity to be known:

Frank: I feel I can understand you and - God, I've been with you long enough if you talk at all (laughter), you know, I recognize your nuances. I recognize your body language. That's what I like. You have to be with somebody for a long time before you can recognize those things, and I really don't think you can really know somebody really well unless you're married to them...I mean you know more about me than most people...! mean you can anticipate my moods.

At the second interview 4 years after the first interview, Frank reflected on the benefits of marriage retrospectively, as his wife, Shelly, had died the previous year to brain cancer:

Frank: If you can find somebody and you can tell them things about yourself that are not very attractive, if you can trust them enough to do that, and they love you and support you anyway and stand by your loyally anyway, you really have something That's a tremendous thing. There's really nothing else like it in the world. You can't get it in therapy. You can't get it in a store or anywhere else. I initially) thought it (marriage) was all about good sex. Kind of shallow, I know, but I was younger. It doesn't take long for that to wear off. We had sex and as time went on we actually made love, which was kind of a departure for me. Lovemaking is better than sex. They're not even in the same universe.

Wendy (#3) suggested that another benefit of marriage is that it should be: Wendy: a place where the real mean world doesn't have to exit, where there is some refuge. Some sense of rest and peace and a certain way of things operating that things aren't always chaotic, always cruel or insensitive.

Priority of the relationship.

These couples expressed how important it was to view the relationship above personal goals. To Mike, this was a reason for him and Kelly to get together in the first place: together that made "more of a person" than they did separately; that is, the whole is more than the sum of its parts. This attitude would have an impact on decision making for the partners in the relationship. For example, Frank (#4) said;

Frank: I make a decision based on what's best for the family, and I can honestly say that's not always what's best for my own selfish pleasure. I think the minute you start making those decisions based on yourself rather than the higher concept of family, you're taking the first step away from each other. I really do. I think that.

For Frank, this meant changing careers from work in the media where he excelled in sales so that they could settle as a family in one place and not have to move all of the time.

This was a significant personal sacrifice for Frank on behalf of the others in the family.

Jim (#1) also made his career decisions based on what he thought was the overriding welfare of the family. Unfortunately, for him, his wife did not share his opinion on exactly was the family's welfare. She would have gladly given up some creative comforts and financial security to spend more time with her husband.

Fidelity and commitment.

If the marriage were to survive there needed to be a sense of protection around it from outside threats. None of the couples in this sample expressed problems with affairs. The two couples who separated for a time during their relationship did so for other reasons. Vi who lived in a separate residence from her husband said, "I wouldn't think of going out with another man. I wouldn't be interested in anybody else." Harry and Lora (#9), who were separated for long times because of Harry's work said that neither of them was looking for opportunities. They suggested the opportunities for being unfaithful were certainly there if they looked for them, but they actively chose to not put themselves in harm's way, nor did they worry that if the other was looking or not. This act of faithfulness placed the relationship at their center, which they chose to protect instead of seeking out immediate and temporary sources of personal satisfaction that would have been a threat to the relationship.

The elevation of faith over the relationship

For all of the couples in the sample, the relationship was primary over individual wishes. For several couples, this was extended to embrace the belief that God's calling was

primary over the relationship. Thus, for them, there was a kind of hierarchy.

Faith was not a major factor for all the couples. Indeed two couples had opposing religious values. Jim (#1) went to church for superstitious reasons ("That's hick. That's why you go to church every Sunday." and "Why we go to church every Sunday and pray things work out and somehow they do."), while his wife did so because of her faith. George (#6)wanted nothing to do with church, so Vi ended up going alone. Nick and Angie (#5)had been rejected by church people and while they didn't indicate they had rejected their beliefs, their faith in religious people was certainly shattered.

Several couples indicated that their views of God affected how they saw the relationship. For example, Bruce (#3) said that he felt a higher calling from God in his marital relationship, that he was not only responsible to his wife, but also God, to his religious community and to the wider world, to demonstrate a marriage that was worthy of that calling.

He also felt his relationship with God kept him accountable in his relationship with his wife.

If Wendy was unlovable, and he had a hard time loving back, he would remember that God had called him to love his wife. When asked about this concept 3 years and one child after his first interview Bruce said:

Bruce: The elevation of faith over the relationship takes pre-eminence because there's still a lot of selfishness in me. And I will subsume try interests to the relationship sometimes. There's also a lot of self there are good amounts of selfishness. That being married to Wendy is part of my living out of the truth and being obedient to the Lord and so that's what makes me come back and apologize to Wendy so frequently and to even do other things that I don't really enjoy, like doing dishes and being involved around the house, taking care of Wendy. We're expecting another child in

November and Wendy's been really pretty worthless the last two weeks (because of the pregnancy). I don't really want to take care of Wendy sometimes, when she's not feeling well I'm busy and tired as she is and so those things are important, but the elevation of faith...knowing that it is the right thing to do is even more important.

Frank (#4) agreed, suggesting that by being faithful to his wife by taking care of her and his son, he was fulfilling God's call upon his life which had its own reward.

The wives of these two men viewed the things that happened to them as a couple as part of God's larger plan. Shelly (#4) viewed her early pregnancy with wonder, believing it was a miracle. Even though they did not have the money for a new baby, she did not doubt that with God's help, they would be able to work things out.

Shelly: I felt that God had actually given us this child. Because the odds were so against me...For so long that they had told (me) there was a good chance that I never would (have a child). I just felt that (even though)...it was a wrong time, I guess my belief always was, we'll work it out. I don't know how the money's going to come in, but it'll come. And that was the belief that God had given us this child and that things would work out.

Wendy (#3) interpreted the domestic violence she was experiencing as NOT God's will. She prayed to God to ask him to intervene, to change her, to change Bruce, to change their relationship. The couple viewed the changes they made to make the relationship safe as done through God's help, thus affirming their faith in God and each other.

Two couples mentioned the intact of the church on their marriage. Frank (#4) attributed his embrace of faith as key to their remarriage. He began attending church during his separation to find a deeper meaning to his existence. He had rejected faith, God, and the church his entire life as being superstitious and irrelevant. Attending church as a family and being involved in a community of faith involved them in a regular ritual each week that gave them stability as a couple and the support of a larger community. They did not just go to church, they became involved in the church so that they were able to build relationships with others. It is also interesting that Shelly was able to sacrifice her own personal faith preference, having been raised a Catholic, to attend a Protestant Church with her husband, to save the marriage and for the benefit of her son.

For Bruce and Wendy, the influence they have felt from the church was through personal relationships with others within the church. Early in their marriage, Bruce was studying in seminary. After his domestic abuse of his wife, a classmate intervened so that Bruce ended up being accountable to his major professor over the issue which led to counseling for him and the couple. After graduation and a move to another new community and work in a doctoral program, Bruce had a close relationship with several other men in the church. They would meet for the express purpose of helping each other in their lives and they would consistently ask each other every week when they met how they were showing their wives that they cared. The example of these other men and a little chastening here and there were instrumental for Bruce to become a more caring husband.

Bruce: When I was meeting with some guys and we were talking about how we're accountable to one another for a lot of our behaviors and one of the areas as a group we sought to Improve upon was how we related to our wives concerning gentleness and that was good.

Wendy: I think that all improved.

Bruce: We'd ask one another what we had done that week to let our wives know that they were facial Wendy, his wife, suggested that Bruce quit living with her as if he were a bachelor! She felt it was as if he finally matured to the point where he began to act like a husband. For example, Bruce had started too many house projects that he was unable to finish while being so busy with his doctoral program. His men's friends from church helped him on the projects and commented to Bruce that he was trying to do too much. This helped him see that he was going overboard and that his wife had been right in her comments all along. Wendy also reported receiving considerable support from a group of women in the church who helped her through some dark days.

Domain 3. A sense of reciprocity in most of the areas of the relationship

Proposition IV suggested that the greater the perceived equality in exchange between spouses (reciprocity), the greater the likelihood that low-quality marriage will remain stable. This proposition was found to hold for all the couples, so much so, that a new corollary can be added that "the more areas of the relationship that are perceived to be reciprocal, the more the marital quality."

This was again seen in the separation of the couples into two groups: 7 of 9 who saw a relative balance of give and take in most of the areas of their relationship versus the 2 couples who expressed discontent in this area (couples #6, married 31 years and #1, married 27 years). In both of these latter couples, the wives were the ones who expressed inequity. Debbie (#1) expressed it in the areas of partnership, time together, decision making, and sharing of household duties. Vi (#6) expressed it mostly in the area of time together, which was not about to happen because of Vi's abhorrence of being alone with George and George's abhorrence of being with Vi in the presence of others.

Domain 4. An ability to adapt to each other and their circumstances

Two propositions addressed the nature of developmental change in the marriage relationship and this effect upon stability. Proposition VII suggested that the greater the individual plasticity in one or both spouses, the greater the likelihood a low-quality couple will remain stable and Proposition VIII suggested that as multidirectional increases, stability increases. That is, to the extent that couples can replace areas of deficit with pluses in other areas their stability will increase.

Plasticity was discussed as the ability of a person to adapt to changing circumstances and to make up for deficits, either through outside intervention or through compensating in other areas. Multidirectionality, on the other hand, was defined as the idea that throughout the life span people vary in the direction of their functioning. An example of plasticity would be if a spouse was unhappy in one area of the marriage, elevating another area of the marriage to meet the happiness deficit.

An example of multidirectionality would be if the marriage wasn't working that well, for the spouse or the couple to find other ways to find fulfillment.

Plasticity was found in all the couples in the sample. By definition, each of the couples was discontent in some way in the relationship as their DAS scores were lower than the population of the rest of the couples. Each was able to find other things in the relationship that gave them personal satisfaction, such as their shared interest in their children or grandchildren and their friendship with each other. A particular area that gave satisfaction for most of the couples was the idea that the current status of the relationship did not mean that the rest of the relationship would stay at that level There was a hope for most that over time the relationship would continue to improve.

Interestingly, for the couples where plasticity was important, multidirectionality was not as important and for the couples where plasticity was not important, multirectionality was important. The two couples who reported little change and adaptation also reported that they had other things to occupy their time. Jim and Debbie (couple #1) both kept busy in their own spheres: Jim in his work and Debbie in her job and circle of network outside the relationship. George and Vi (couple # 6), who was retired, had opted for separate lifestyles, living in separate homes with George spending time in the outdoors, hunting and fishing, and spending time talking with her friends. Both of these spheres gave them individual enjoyment, but at the same time reminded them of their vastly different interests. The other couples did not report multidirectionality and wanted to work things out together. While not specifically asked, one would anticipate that the other 7 couples would see multidirectionality as a deficit and taking away from their efforts to become partners in the relationship.

Two couples expressed pessimism about the future (married 27 and 31 years). The rest of the couples were positive about their future. The optimism of these seven couples was in stark contrast to the pessimism of the two couples. Is there a relationship between satisfaction in the relationship and the amount of anticipated positive change in the fixture envisioned by the couple? Perhaps the reason the other seven couples were in the low DAS scores compared to the other 91 couples in the larger sample is that the younger couples were still recovering from the conflict between them in the early years of the relationship. For example, two individuals expressed that despite the tremendous strides their partner had made in their years together, they still had their doubts and struggled with trusting that their partner had made genuine changes. How long would these people have to wait until their trust had been built up enough to improve their overall outlook for the relationship? Thus, it appears that the seven couples had lower DAS scores for different reasons than the two long-term couples.

Much of the change in the relationship described in the "Results" chapter seemed to be related to individual maturity. For example, becoming more assertive, less demanding, more responsible, less argumentative, more open to a spouse's input, improved listening produce dramatically improved interaction effects with resulting positive feelings about the possibility of the relationship. While on the surface these would be observed as couple changes, they might also be attributed to individuals differentiating and learning to treat each other with more dignity and respect, Individuals being willing to change and adapt mean that their relationships will also change.

It is interesting to note that couple conflict management styles do not change for couples. However, in this book, several couples indicated a change in how they interacted and deal with conflict.

Domain 5. Attitude toward the limitations of each other and the relationship

Proposition V suggested that as the relationship changes and expectations of one or both spouses are not met, one or both will likely adjust their expectations and thus increase the likelihood that the marriage system will remain stabilized. Adjusted expectations were true for nearly all of the couples. Adjusted expectations led to acceptance. This experience also improved marital quality. All but 2 of the couples reported making adjustments to each other. Two couples did not indicate that change or adjusted expectations were instrumental in their stability. They were stable without these characteristics. However, this would not seem to be normal for most couples in our culture where an emphasis on couple satisfaction is so important.

Proposition VI suggested that the more the changes in expectations and choices of spouses are congruent, the greater the probability that marital stability will remain at the status quo level. Congruency was divided again between the

7 couples who were congruent in most areas and 2 couples who were not congruent. Of the 7 couples who expressed congruency in most areas, one individual (Nick couple #5, married 7 years)indicated that he separated and was serious about filing for divorce from Angie because he did not feel his wife had the same expectations as he did about emotional involvement.

When Angie was willing to align her expectations and behavior (choices) more in sync with Nick, they were able to reunite and make considerable strides in their relationship.

Another couple reported that Mike's (couple #2) decision (choice) for Kelly to get an abortion had negative effects upon their marital quality. However, as devastating as this choice was, it was not a threat to the relationship, only to marital quality.

Still another couple (#3, Bruce and Wendy) said that even though their first year was marred by Bruce's choice to use domestic violence against Wendy, Wendy was determined to make the marriage work and to stay married. Bruce's choice did not affect Wendy's commitment to stay married.

Many couples indicated that they chose to stay faithful to each other which had a bearing on their long-term commitment. It is not known, however, whether there were other negative choices that spouses made that were or were not a threat to the marriage. It is doubtful that all negative choices (e.g. affairs, criminal behavior, gambling, etc.) would come to light in one or two interviews (for further elaboration on the limits of the qualitative method used in this study see that section later in this chapter).

In this study, then, for most couples, it would seem that congruency in expectations and choices would be more a prediction of marital quality than stability.

Reformulating a typology of LQHS couples

Earlier this paper suggested that LQHS couples were different than high-quality-high stability couples because, for the former, marital quality was not an issue for their stability, but for the latter it was. Stability for both HQHS couples and LQHS couples is the same prerequisite for marital quality. It could be, however, that there are two types of HQHS couples: 1) those that will remain high stability regardless of the level of marital quality, and 2) those Also will move to HQLS or LQLS should their perceived marital quality deteriorate. In the former group stability may serve as a prerequisite for marital quality; in the latter group perceived marital quality will determine the level of stability.

The characteristics of Enduring Couples are close to couples who are highly distressed and in our culture highly prone to divorce. Perhaps in other cultures with stronger social mores against divorce, this type of couple may be more prevalent.

However, in this culture, with its strong emphasis on rewarding relationships, it would appear that most couples that enter the enduring type would be likely soon to wear out and end up in divorce.

Results

This book looked at the actors low-quality couples say contribute to their staying together as couples. These are couples who decide to stay together regardless of their marital quality. In this qualitative sample of 18 individuals (9 couples) only one person indicated that her marital stability was linked to marital quality. Even this one woman, who had been married twice before, did not anticipate getting a divorce from her third husband, because for her the marital quality was sufficiently high. For the rest of the subjects, divorce was not an option.

This book discovered that in low-quality couples there are two trajectories. One trajectory was where change is not anticipated, leaving the couple to stand together in perseverance. They "endured" the situation for the welfare of the marriage. These couples (2married 27 and 31 years) were marked by the lack of partnership between spouses, a lack of agreement on decision making, and little fondness for each other. The second trajectory was marked by younger couples who still had hope that things would change for them and between them in the future because they had witnessed a change of some sort hi the relationship already. These Striving Couples (7 of 9) reported being happier in their relationship, shared more in decision making, and tended to be able to accept or were working on accepting the shortcomings of their partner.

While all the couples reported immediate setbacks early in their relationship (such as early pregnancy, abortion, financial problems, career problems, disagreements on career choices, health, and mental health issues, domestic violence, in-laws, drop-in social support)and were able to endure these setbacks, only the 7 couples mentioned above were able to move beyond these setbacks to begin to heal the relationship. For them, marital quality was still important and worth their effort.

All 7 of these couples reported making conscious efforts to making their relationships better. The latter 2 couples reached a certain marital quality plateau from which they were never able to rise. The wives of these 2 husbands reported making considerable efforts to improve their marriages. The husbands of these two wives reported that these efforts were viewed as meddling and negative. These two husbands were not open to the influence of their wives. By the time of the interview, each partner had given up the idea of their relationships improving.

Intervention with unstable couples in couple therapy

What about those couples who marry with high ideals and high relationship quality, reach a major obstacle or series of obstacles, and then seek divorce early in the relationship?

It would appear that these couples have NOT learned the survival skills of Enduring or striving Couples and end up assuming that the downward spiral they are on can only get worse. Thus, therapeutic intervention with these couples would seek to instill these skills in the couple.

Those couples unable to endure the difference between their expectations and the reality of their relationship and who are resistant to making changes necessary to change personally or to receive input from their partner would be viewed as those who are highly likely to divorce. Thus, for couples struggling with issues of bitterness and resentment, acceptance may be too distant a goal for the initial stages of therapy.

A more achievable goal might be to help them move toward endurance. On the other, hand couples who come to therapy who are in the "enduring" stage may need to learn to not take the actions of their partner as personal affronts and to accept influence from their partner Movement in these two areas would be critical steps in helping acquiescent couples move toward acceptance.

Many of the distressed couples who come to therapy often do so in the early stages of marriage and find the challenges before them as too stressful, bringing their marital system to the breaking point. This research would suggest that the first item of business of the therapist in this type of situation would be to assist the couple in overcoming these challenges and to help them unite against then foes, whatever they may be.

While certainly some divorce for purely self-centered and self-serving reasons, the experience of the researcher as a therapist is that most people who are struggling in their marriage do not seek divorce as an option until they have reached a pain threshold where the relationship seems unbearable. They do not have or do not want to have the endurance to simply bear through an unrewarding relationship. They have no desire to stay in the "enduring" mode. However, most say that if there is some movement toward the characteristics listed on the "striving" side, that would be enough to keep them going. The key elemental difference between enduring and striving couples seems to be movement. Enduring couples are locked in an unchanging stasis that eliminates hope from their repertoire, meaning that they either decide that the current pattern is bearable for the rest of their human lives, or they divorce. In this case, stability is dichotomous.

But for striving couples, words like "hope," "change," "maturity," kept reoccurring.

They were not content to stay at a level where the relationship did not seem to be working.

Interestingly, for all 7 of these couples, each partner was making an effort to change themselves or how they interacted to improve the marriage. Thus, a key intervention strategy would be to look for how the couple had changed together over their time as a couple, how they had been open to the other's influence, how they had tried to reach out and meet the other person's needs, and in what way they had sacrificed then: own happiness for the benefit of the other. Perhaps these characteristics are present in the relationship but overshadowed by the level of stress the couple is facing at the time they come to therapy. Reminding the couple of these strengths and helping them to harness them in times of need may help them triumph over their obstacles.

In closing, this book aims to achieve couples goals not splashing in an uncommunicative and in a psychological individual shutting. Helping each other, to rise together and mutually from our own shallows.

This book has investigated the question of what keeps low quality-high stability couples together. It was suggested that the normal method of study of marriage, using marital quality as a predictor of marital stability, would not be relevant for LQHS couples who have decided to stay married regardless of their marital quality. It was also decided to use a qualitative methodology to ferret out the characteristics of LQHS couples, since this research question, while suggestive was not directly approached in the marital literature.

A model was postulated based upon the research literature that suggested two trajectories for low-quality couples: one where marital quality gradually increases over time and one where marital quality plateaus or drops over time. Nine propositions were made about the nature of stability in LQHS couples based upon a review of the literature and appropriate theoretical orientations.

Qualitative interviews with 9 couples married 5 years or longer who scored the lowest on the DAS out of a larger sample of 99 couples were used for the investigation. The couples varied in length of marriage from 5 to 31 years. The interviews were transcribed and studied.

Five domains were discovered that LQHS couples suggest are characteristics that determine their stability as couples. Appropriate qualitative techniques, including peer review, were utilized to assure the trustworthiness of the methodology.

It was found that the couples in this sample had considerable struggles early in their marriages that tended to serve as a bonding factor for them. The challenges ranged from career and money problems, in-laws, bosses and children, health, and domestic violence. It was also found that all of the couples viewed the marriage as more important than individuality, expressed in such areas as their belief that divorce was not an option, their belief in the benefits of marriage, the priority of the relationship, and their commitment to faithfulness in the relationship.

From here the couples diverged into two types called hi this dissertation Striving Couples and Enduring Couples. Striving Couples (N=7) were defined as those who were making movement and efforts to improve their marital quality. Enduring Couples (N=2) were locked in an unchanging pattern that convinced the couple that improvement in marital quality was not to be expected.

Striving and Enduring Couples had different approaches to the final three domains.

Reciprocity was a critical aspect of Striving Couples, but not Enduring Couples. Striving Couples invested time and energy in encouraging the good things in the relationship (fun, friendship), sought to meet each other's needs, and made an effort to work together as a partnership. Striving Couples also made an effort to adapt to each other and their circumstances and viewed their relationship as changing drastically since the early stages of their relationship. They were open to change and viewed it as a reason to give them hope to face the future. Change in how they communicated with each other was crucial as Striving Couples were able to adapt to less conflictual patterns of interaction. Enduring Couples had the same general patterns of interaction throughout their marriage and did not anticipate that would change. Striving Couples shared decision-making responsibilities, whereas in Enduring Couples the decisions were either made by the husband or made individually, with no regard for partnership. All of the couples had to deal with shattered expectations, but Striving Couples tended to move toward acceptance of their partner's limitations, be open to their partner's influence in their lives, and respect their partner.

Enduring Couples acquiesced about their partner's limitations, that is, they endured them, but did not like the limitations and tended to let those limitations bother them personality. As a result, they were unable or unwilling to accept influence from their partner nor to respect them.

Several couples in the sample were able to move beyond acceptance to contentment with their situation and lot in life.

The domains were then integrated into the nine propositions, the theoretical and empirical research literature review. The five domains and two couple types supported the initial model delineated in the theory chapter. A new model was created that suggested that for low-quality couples, both marital quality and marital stability are on a continuum.

Divorcing Couples, on the left of the continuum, were those couples who had exceed their pain threshold with such characteristics as change for the worst, instability, resentment, and low marital quality. Enduring Couples, in the middle of the continuum, were those who "endured" their relationship pain but had not been able to make peace with it. They were characterized as unchanging in interactional patterns, tending toward acquiescence in their attitudes toward their partner's limitations, and had low marital quality. The third group of couples, on the right of the continuum of low-quality couples, were Striving Couples, characterized as those who had made peace or were in process of making peace with the pain they had experienced in the relationship. They were learning to accept their partner's limitations by adjusting their expectations of one another. They were more open to their partner's influence and tended to respect their partner. As a result, while their marital quality was still low, they improved in their marital quality.

Clinical implications based on this continuum were explored including a suggested assessment instrument for measuring stability in low-quality couples and possible intervention strategies.

It is concluded that LQHS couples, indeed, have much to teach researchers, clinicians, and other couples about their particular view of reality that emphasizes the stability of the marriages despite low marital quality. They have many positive qualities that are worth emulating and that should apply to other couples who desire to stay married despite heavy odds that they may feel weigh against them.

CPSIA information can be obtained
at www.ICGtesting.com
Printed in the USA
BVHW091407231120
593971BV00002B/438